I0812635

The INSIDE GUIDE

STEM IN SPORTS

STEM in Basketball

By Beatrice Harris

Cavendish Square

Published in 2025 by Cavendish Square Publishing, LLC
2544 Clinton Street Buffalo, NY 14224

Website: cavendishsq.com

Library of Congress Cataloging-in-Publication Data

Names: Harris, Beatrice, author.
Title: STEM in basketball / Beatrice Harris.
Description: Buffalo, New York : Cavendish Square Publishing, [2025] | Series: The inside guide: STEM in sports | Includes index. | Audience: Grades 4-6
Identifiers: LCCN 2023049188 (print) | LCCN 2023049189 (ebook) | ISBN 9781502671257 (library binding) | ISBN 9781502671240 (paperback) | ISBN 9781502671264 (ebook)
Subjects: LCSH: Basketball–Juvenile literature. | Science–Study and teaching–Juvenile literature. | Sports sciences–Juvenile literature.
Classification: LCC GV885.1 .H375 2025 (print) | LCC GV885.1 (ebook) | DDC 796.323–dc23/eng/20231101
LC record available at https://lccn.loc.gov/2023049188
LC ebook record available at https://lccn.loc.gov/2023049189

Editor: Therese Shea
Copyeditor: Danielle Haynes
Designer: Deanna Lepovich

The photographs in this book are used by permission and through the courtesy of: Cover Vasyl Shulga/Shutterstock.com; p. 4 Lopolo/Shutterstock.com; p. 6 zhangjin_net/Shutterstock.com; p. 7 SPP Sport Press Photo./Alamy Stock Photo; p. 8 Anucha Tiemsom/Shutterstock.com; p. 9 PHILIPPE MONTIGNY/Shutterstock.com; p. 10 Valentin Valkov/Shutterstock.com; p. 11 Gorodenkoff/Shutterstock.com; p. 12 Oleksandr Osipov/Shutterstock.com; p. 14 LightField Studios/Shutterstock.com; p. 15 Jon Chica/Shutterstock.com; p. 16 claudiuslower82/Shutterstock.com; p. 18 topimages/Shutterstock.com; p. 19 (main) leungchopan/Shutterstock.com; p. 19 (inset) UPI/Alamy Stock Photo; p. 21 Chris Poss/Alamy Stock Photo; p. 22 Ververidis Vasilis/Shutterstock.com; p. 24 JoeSAPhotos/Shutterstock.com; p. 25 Nadir Keklik/Shutterstock.com; p. 26 Andrey Burmakin/Shutterstock.com; p. 27 Sergey Ryzhov/Shutterstock.com; p. 28 (top) Alex Kravtsov/Shutterstock.com; p. 28 (bottom) PhotoProCorp/Shutterstock.com; p. 29 (top) Dmitry SKilkov/Shutterstock.com; p. 29 (bottom) ACHPF/Shutterstock.com.

CPSIA compliance information: Batch #CSCSQ25: For further information contact Cavendish Square Publishing LLC at 1-877-980-4450.

Printed in the United States of America

CONTENTS

All you need to play basketball are a ball, a hard surface, and one or two baskets.

Chapter One

A STEM SPORT

A game called "basket ball" was invented in Springfield, Massachusetts, in 1891. That sport is now wildly popular all over the world. Even people who don't follow basketball closely know of its superstars, such as Diana Taurasi, LeBron James, and Stephen Curry.

Both the kids on a neighborhood court and the professionals in a huge **arena** rely on STEM ideas to get the ball into the basket. STEM—short for science, **technology**, engineering, and math—are four fields that help us understand the sport of basketball and have an impact on how it's played. They aid us in answering questions, such as how to score points and what shoes work best on the court.

Fast Fact

In the United States, the top pro basketball leagues are the National Basketball Association (NBA) and the Women's National Basketball Association (WNBA).

Starting with Stats

Let's begin with the M of STEM—math! Numbers are an important part of every game of basketball. Numbers help people compare players and teams. Statistics, sometimes just called stats, are numbers that represent pieces of

Studying free throw percentage stats can help players know if they need to practice harder at the free throw line.

information. Without stats, we'd never know which team is winning or which player has scored the most points.

Other types of stats that people collect about pro basketball include numbers of **rebounds**, steals, and blocks. These are recorded per game, per season, and per career. Another stat is field goal percentage. This is found by dividing a player's (or team's) number of successful shots by the total number of shots taken. Free throw percentage is found in a similar way.

Size and Shape

All NBA courts are the same shape and size. The rectangle that makes up an NBA court has two sides that are 94 feet (28.7 meters) long and

Fast Fact

The branch of math that deals with measurements, shapes, lines, and points is called geometry.

The WNBA court is the same size as the NBA court, but the distance from the 3-point line to the basket is slightly shorter.

two sides that are 50 feet (15.2 m) long. Within the larger rectangle are many other lines that help players know where they should be. For example, each NBA court has two 3-point lines, with one on each end of the

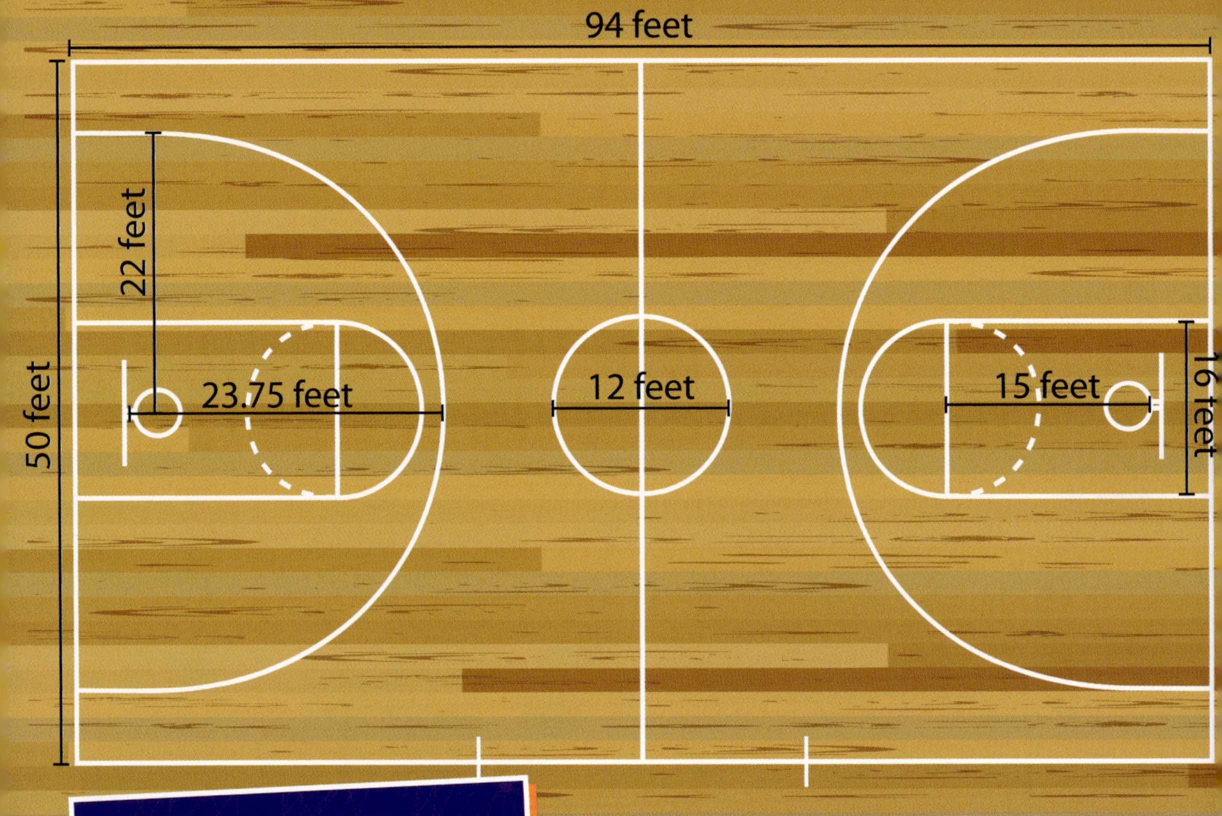

Fast Fact

The 3-point line isn't a true semicircle. It becomes a straight line when it nears the court's edge and is 22 feet (6.7 m) from the basket at that point.

NBA players practice shots and plays according to the court measurements shown above.

court. These lines make a sort of semicircle, or half circle.

The basket lies where you would find the center if the semicircle was a whole circle. The distance from a spot on most of the 3-point line to the basket is 23.75 feet (7.2 m). This is called the arc radius. Arc radius measures the distance from the center of a circle to a point on an arc of that circle. NBA players get an extra point if they successfully shoot a basket from beyond the semicircle.

NOTHING BUT NET

Much of the action on a basketball court takes place around the basket, which is sometimes called the net. The circular metal hoop that holds up the net is called the rim. Basketball rims have a diameter of 18 inches (45.7 centimeters). The diameter is the measurement of any straight line that passes through the center of a circle. If the diameter of the rim was even an inch larger, it would be easier to make a shot. This is because a circle expands in every direction as its diameter increases.

A basketball is about 9 inches (22.9 cm) in diameter, or half the diameter of the hoop.

It's not always possible to put the ball directly into the net with a dunk. Physics is at work to make the ball soar through the air and into the hoop.

Chapter Two

PHYSICS IS THE STAR

Physics is a branch of science that has to do with physical matter and how forces and energy affect it. Both forces and energy are an important part of basketball.

A force is a push or pull on an object. You can find examples of forces all over a basketball court. When a player shoots the basketball, they're pushing the ball with their hands. This is an example of applied force. Applied force is a force

Fast Fact

The force of gravity pulls down a basketball after a player shoots it into the air.

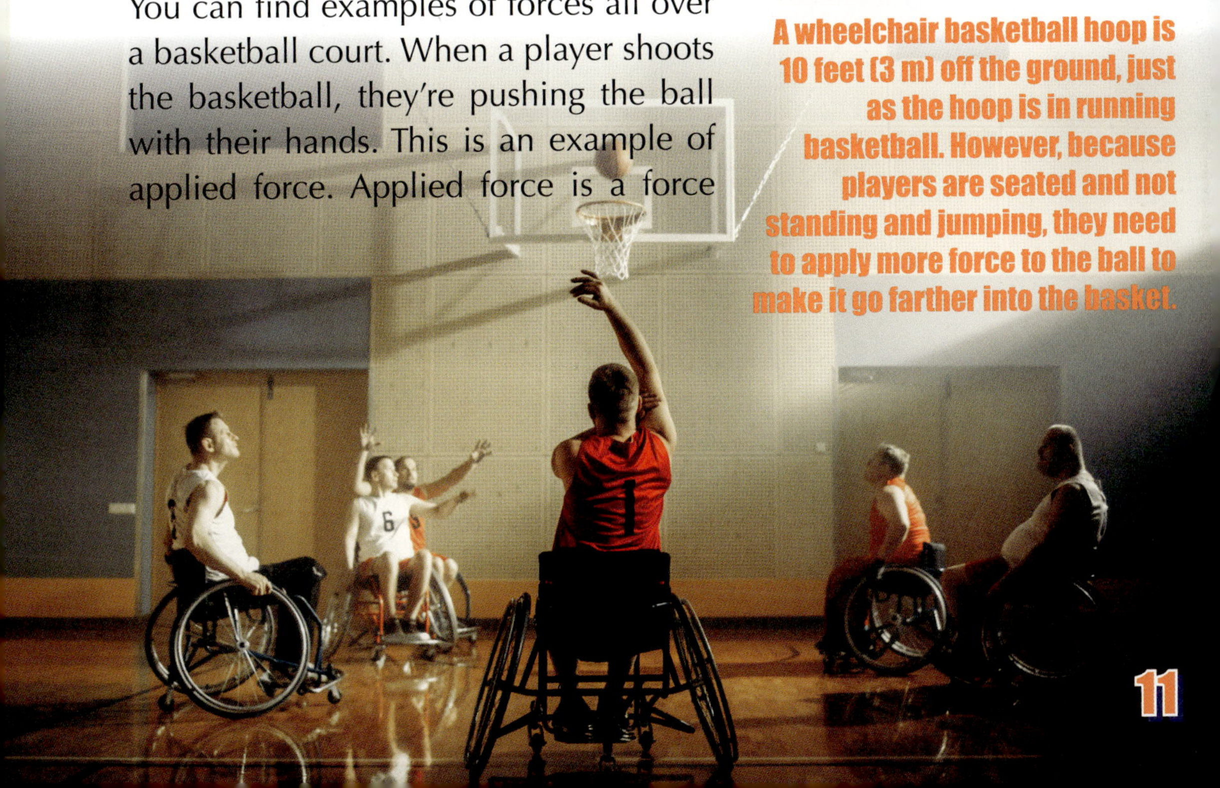

A wheelchair basketball hoop is 10 feet (3 m) off the ground, just as the hoop is in running basketball. However, because players are seated and not standing and jumping, they need to apply more force to the ball to make it go farther into the basket.

one object **exerts** on another. How are force and energy connected? You need energy to apply force!

Motion on the Court

Most pro basketball players are tall. They also have a lot of muscle mass. The heavier a player is, the more mass they have. Mass is how much matter is in an object. Mass is like

Fast Fact

Did you know the ground exerts a force too? When basketball players stand on the court, the court is exerting an upward force to support them. That force is called normal force.

Sometimes players can't keep their momentum from taking them out of bounds.

weight, but an object's weight depends on gravity. A basketball player might weigh 200 pounds (91 kilograms) on Earth, but they would weigh something else on another planet that has a different amount of gravity. The player's mass, however, will always be the same.

> **Fast Fact**
>
> Use math to figure out momentum! Multiply mass by **velocity**. Momentum is measured in units called kilogram meters per second or newton-seconds. Direction is also a part of the answer.

Momentum is the word for mass in motion. The more mass an object has, the harder it is for it to slow down and stop. It takes more force to change the motion of an object with more mass, so it's harder for bigger basketball players to start running, stop, and change direction.

Forces on the Court

The surface of a basketball court can make a big difference in how a ball bounces. Basketball players must dribble, or bounce, the ball as they move. A ball will bounce back with the most force on a hard surface. Soft surfaces absorb more of the ball's energy, so it doesn't bounce back with as much force. This is why basketballs don't bounce well on grassy surfaces.

Professional and **collegiate** basketball teams play on hardwood floors, often made from the wood of maple trees. A hardwood floor is a strong and smooth surface that doesn't absorb too much of the ball's energy when it's dribbled. This makes it the ideal surface for basketball games.

ATHLETIC TRAINING

Basketball players' genes are responsible for their height. However, they're not born with their power and skills. That comes from training. They build muscles so they have the strength to make baskets, beat their opponent down the court, and block shots. Professional trainers help athletes build muscles with the actions of their sport in mind. They must know a lot about the human body to do this. Anatomy is the study of body structures, such as muscles, bones, lungs, and the heart. Physiology is the study of how these body parts work.

Trainers can also teach players exercises that help prevent injuries.

Concrete and asphalt courts are so hard that they're tough on a player's body over time—especially their bones and joints. However, many pros started learning the game on their neighborhood outdoor courts.

Hardwood floors are used only for indoor basketball courts as weather can ruin them. Outdoor courts are made with concrete or asphalt. These strong, hard materials absorb even less energy from the bouncing ball.

Thanks to technology like this, spectators don't have to keep score at a basketball game themselves. They can also watch the game on TV or the internet.

LET'S TALK ABOUT TECH

Chapter Three

Basketball, especially pro basketball, makes use of technology, such as scoreboards, cameras, and video. One kind of technology is video replay. This lets officials look more closely at a play in the game when they're unsure what happened. Often, the play is captured by several camera angles for a better view. The play might be the difference between a win and a loss, so the video is important.

However, other kinds of basketball technology don't have to do with electronics at all. You're probably using some of this technology when you play!

Footwear?

That's right—shoes are technology! Basketball shoes help players perform better. The material on the bottom of shoes provides friction. Friction is any force that resists motion. It occurs when objects make contact.

Why is friction good for basketball players? Often, they must run quickly down

Fast Fact

When pro basketball players fall on the court, you'll see someone wipe up sweat they leave behind. Sweat, water, or any other liquid reduces the amount of friction, causing players to slip.

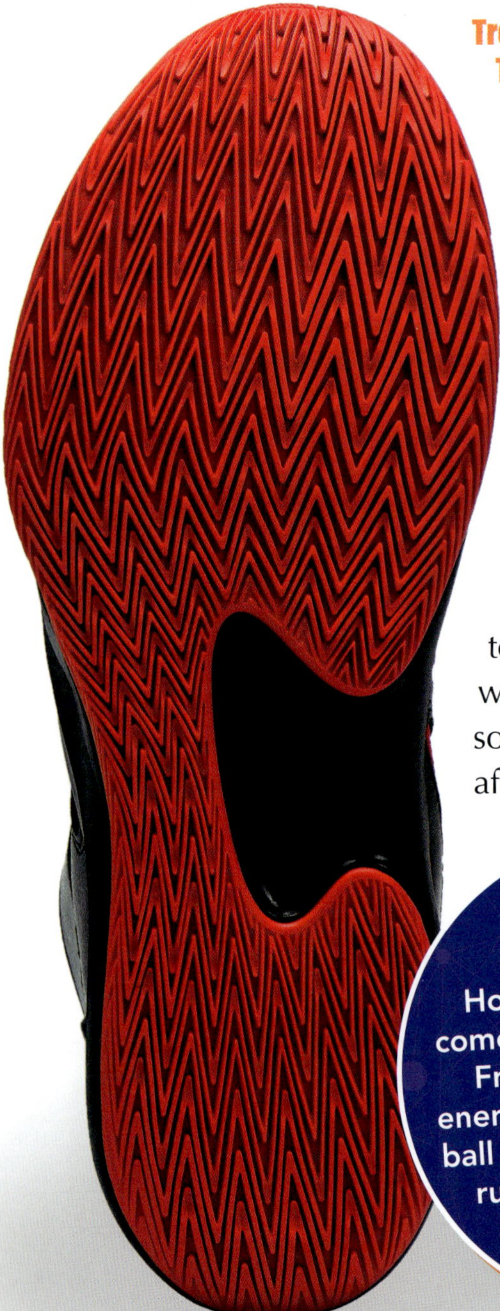

Treads on sneakers are like treads on tires. They provide increased friction.

the court, and friction keeps them from sliding on the smooth surface of the floor. Friction slows the movement of a player's shoe over the floor enough to keep them from slipping and missing a play or even injuring themselves.

The technology used to make and design basketball shoes has improved greatly since the sport's earliest days. Engineers select materials to make shoes as light as possible, while still being strong enough to absorb some of the force when a player lands after jumping.

Fast Fact

How does a basketball come in contact with heat? Friction gives off heat energy as molecules on the ball and the court's surface rub against each other and begin to move faster.

What About the Ball?

The ball, too, is engineered to be the best kind of ball for the game. The friction between a player's hands and the basketball wears down the surface of the ball over time. This is because basketballs are often made of leather, which softens as it's exposed to heat and friction.

In 2006, the NBA allowed the use of a composite basketball. It didn't need to be broken in like a leather ball does. However, the players didn't like the feel of the composite balls, so they returned to leather ones that same season.

The tiny bumps on a basketball's surface are called pebbling. They help create friction between a player's hands and the ball for better ball handling.

AIR CAN BE A DRAG

Another name for air resistance is drag. Picture air molecules striking the surface of the basketball as it's in the air. This happens whenever a player passes or shoots the ball. Air resistance increases as an object's velocity increases. In basketball, air resistance doesn't have too much of an effect on an inflated ball's path. In other sports, such as baseball and cycling, air resistance has a much more noticeable effect. A special branch of science deals with objects moving through air and air moving around objects. It's called aerodynamics.

Fast Fact

Does your basketball have enough air pressure? Hold the ball up and in front of your head. Let it go. If it bounces up to elbow height, it has enough air pressure.

A basketball is basically a flat piece of material when there's no air inside it. Air is pumped into a basketball through a tiny hole. As more air gets pumped in, the air pressure inside the ball increases. Air pressure is the force exerted on a surface, such as the inside of a basketball, by air molecules.

If the air pressure inside a basketball is too low, it won't bounce well. It also won't hold the round shape of the basketball. Worse, a deflated ball won't travel as far as an inflated one when it's thrown. Instead, it will experience more of a type of friction called air resistance.

NBA and WNBA balls should have an air pressure of 7.5 to 8.5 pounds per square inch (PSI). Other leagues allow slightly lower pressures. A pressure gauge is a tool that can give a precise measurement.

In still shots of the action on a basketball court, players can seem to do superhuman things. Everything can be explained through science, though!

THE LAWS OF THE COURT

Chapter Four

Isaac Newton was a scientist who lived from 1643 to 1727. He defined some basic laws about matter and motion. Today, these are called Newton's laws of motion. They can help us figure out what's happening on the basketball court.

Newton's Laws of Motion

Newton's first law of motion states that an object at rest stays at rest and an object in motion stays in motion at the same velocity unless affected by an outside force. On the court, you see this on display if a ball sits on the floor. It won't move without a force acting on it. A ball in motion, however, will continue to move unless forces act on it, such as being caught by someone, brought down by gravity, or stopped by friction.

> **Fast Fact**
>
> Newton's second law also states that as the mass of an object increases, its acceleration decreases.

Newton's second law of motion is about **acceleration**. It states that an object's acceleration is affected by the forces acting on the object and the mass of the object. If the force acting on an object increases, the object's acceleration increases.

Fast Fact

Pro backboards are made of tempered glass, which is engineered to be shatter-resistant.

Players learn to shoot from different angles and distances with the proper aim and amount of force. A missed shot can bounce away from the net—and into the hands of an opponent.

Imagine a basketball player passing the ball to a teammate. Without enough force, the ball might move too slow and be **intercepted**, or stolen, by an opponent. With more force, the ball will accelerate and reach its target faster.

Newton's third law of motion states that for every action, there's an equal and opposite **reaction**. You can see this at work when a

A BETTER BASKET

Engineers use math, science, and technology to solve problems. One problem on basketball courts years ago was the backboard breaking or the rim bending whenever a player dunked the ball. An assistant basketball coach asked his uncle, Arthur Ehrat, to solve this problem. Ehrat figured out a design for a flexible, or bendable, basketball rim in the late 1970s. He used a spring from a farm machine that allowed the rim to bend and snap back into place when released. Without this kind of rim, modern games would constantly be delayed by shattering backboards and bending rims!

Not all courts have this kind of "breakaway rim," but pro and college courts do.

Sometimes basketball players dunk the ball with so much force that they break the backboard! If they do this on purpose, they'll receive a technical foul.

basketball bounces off a backboard with the same amount of force used to throw it up there.

The Law of Energy

Another law of physics can be applied to the basketball court. It's called the law of conservation of energy. It states that energy can't be created or destroyed. It can only change forms.

The two main categories of energy are potential energy and kinetic energy. Potential energy is stored energy. Kinetic energy is moving energy. When a basketball is resting in your hand above the ground, it has potential energy. As the ball falls to the ground, it has kinetic energy.

STEM Stars

The best basketball players are smart. They might not think about how their skills are rooted in STEM, but they are. Players can always use STEM

When a player dribbles a basketball, some potential energy is changed to heat and sound energy, which are kinds of kinetic energy. The friction between the ball and floor produces heat. We experience the sound energy as the noise of a ball bouncing.

to improve their game—by exercising in a new way, examining their stats, practicing shots from different angles and distances, and checking out the latest athletic gear technology.

You, too, can use STEM knowledge to raise your level of play—and your performance in the classroom. STEM is all around us, and recognizing it in your life can help you achieve your A game!

Fast Fact

The crowds at basketball games can produce a lot of sound! This energy travels as sound waves. Sound waves produce heat energy as they travel, though only a small amount.

THINK ABOUT IT!

1. Think of one more example of how a science, technology, engineering, or math concept is displayed in basketball.

2. How might basketball players use a knowledge of physics to improve their skills?

3. Some people think the technology of video review shouldn't be used in sports. What do you think, and why?

4. What advantages might shorter basketball players have over taller basketball players, according to science?

GLOSSARY

acceleration: The rate at which the velocity of an object in motion changes over time.

arena: A building for sports and other forms of entertainment that has a large central area surrounded by seats.

asphalt: A natural matter often used to make roads.

collegiate: Relating to a college or its students.

composite: A solid made from two or more kinds of matter.

exert: To put forth, as in a force.

intercept: To take control of a pass that was meant for a player on the other team.

reaction: The force that an object subjected to an outside force exerts in the opposite direction.

rebound: A ball recovered off a missed shot.

technical foul: The breaking of a rule that often has to do with unsportsmanlike conduct.

technology: Using science, engineering, and other industries to invent useful tools or to solve problems. Also, a machine, piece of equipment, or method created by technology.

tempered: Describing a material that has been made hard and strong by heating and cooling it.

velocity: The change in the position of an object divided by time. Velocity also includes a direction.

FIND OUT MORE

Books

Kelley, K. C. *Basketball: Score with STEM!* Minneapolis, MN: Bearport Publishing, 2022.

Schaller, Bob. *The Everything Kids' Basketball Book: A Guide to Your Favorite Players and Teams—and Tips on Playing Like a Pro*. New York, NY: Adams Media, 2021.

Ventura, Marne. *Learning STEM from Basketball: Why Does a Basketball Bounce? And Other Amazing Answers for Kids*. New York, NY: Sky Pony Press, 2021.

Websites

Britannica: Basketball
kids.britannica.com/kids/article/basketball/352831
Check out the rules and history of the game.

Tumble: The Physics of Basketball
www.sciencepodcastforkids.com/single-post/2020/03/06/the-physics-of-basketball
Listen to this podcast, and watch videos about physics and sports.

WNBA
www.wnba.com
Read about the Women's National Basketball Association and its stars.

Publisher's note to educators and parents: Our editors have carefully reviewed these websites to ensure that they are suitable for students. Many websites change frequently, however, and we cannot guarantee that a site's future contents will continue to meet our high standards of quality and educational value. Be advised that students should be closely supervised whenever they access the internet.

INDEX